D0849140

ALSO BY CYNTHIA ZARIN

The Ada Poems
The Watercourse
Fire Lyric
The Swordfish Tooth

ESSAYS
An Enlarged Heart: A Personal History

FOR CHILDREN
Saints Among the Animals
Albert, the Dog Who Liked to Ride in Taxis
Wallace Hoskins, the Boy Who Grew Down
Rose and Sebastian
What Do You See When You Shut Your Eyes?

ORBIT

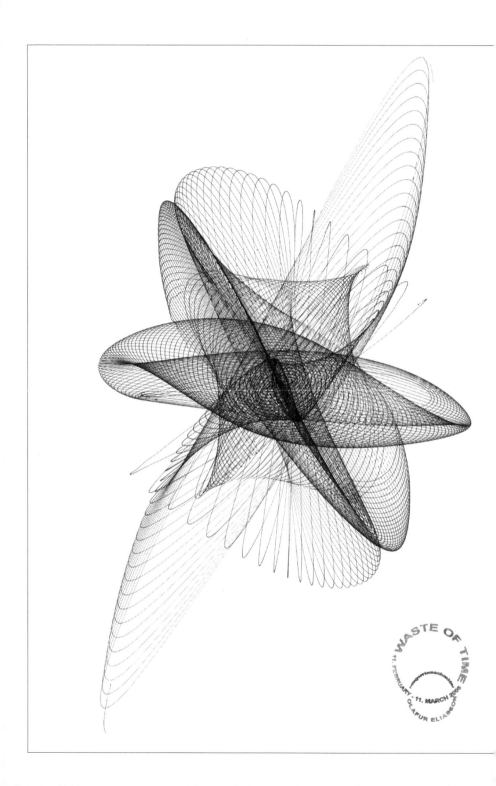

ORBIT

POEMS

CYNTHIA ZARIN

ALFRED A. KNOPF · NEW YORK · 2017

This Is a Borzoi Book Published by Alfred A. Knopf

Copyright © 2017 by Cynthia Zarin

All rights reserved. Published in the United States by Alfred A. Knopf,
a division of Penguin Random House LLC, New York, and
distributed in Canada by Random House of Canada, a division of Penguin Random House
Canada Limited, Toronto.

www.aaknopf.com

Knopf, Borzoi Books, and the colophon are registered trademarks
of Penguin Random House LLC.

Library of Congress Control Number: 2016963050
ISBN 978-0-451-49472-6 (hardcover)
ISBN 978-0-451-49473-3 (ebook)

Jacket design by Peter Mendelsund

Manufactured in the United States of America
First Edition

for Sasha

CONTENTS

3 Flowers

5 Meltwater

6 Faun

7 Mirror

8 Orbit

16 Summer

19 Still Life (for Rose)

20 Anxiety

21 The Impulse Wants Company

27 The Muse of History

31 Three Poems

35 Japanese Poems

36 Blue Vase

37 Sunday

46 Dear and Blackbirds

48 Your Mother Dancing on the Table (Fiesole 1966)

52 Metaphysicks

58 Elbow

59 Conversazione

61 Late Afternoon

62 Class Picture

63 Ouija Board

66 Rainy Day Fugue

75 *Acknowledgments*

ORBIT

FLOWERS

This morning I was walking upstairs
from the kitchen, carrying your
beautiful flowers, the flowers you

brought me last night, calla lilies
and something else, I am not
sure what to call them, white flowers,

of course you had no way of knowing
it has been years since I bought
white flowers—but now you have

and here they are again. I was carrying
your flowers and a coffee cup
and a soft yellow handbag and a book

of poems by a Chinese poet, in
which I had just read the words "come
or go but don't just stand there

in the doorway," as usual I was
carrying too many things, you
would have laughed if you saw me.

It seemed especially important
not to spill the coffee as I usually
do, as I turned up the stairs,

inside the whorl of the house as if
I were walking up inside the lilies.
I do not know how to hold all

the beauty and sorrow of my life.

MELTWATER

A gang of foxes on the wet road, fur
gaggle, the gutter a Ganges, gravel
rutting the glacier's slur and cant. Old proof,
the past can't solve itself, endlessly drawing
its stung logos spirograph. You see
the fox I cannot see; even the children
can see her, vixen and her babies
delicately picking their way along
the white line of the tarmac, the rain
rubbing out their shadows. I want you
as I want water, rain crocheting moss
from mist, sulfur on the pines' crooked limbs,
hapless as the selkie who hums to herself—
no one believes in her but there she is.

FAUN

The faun you can see
    her lariat of bone unfolding

the faun in your arms
    her legs buckled

        moon-mouth

velvet, her breath keyed,
    water

    rasping the bridge
barnacles ringing the pilings
        —black pearls,

the faun's breath spiral,
    circling your head,
    the Horn of Africa

            pausing
    —digitalis,
        cinquefoil, starburst

    pulsing
        to where we walked

        to the end, to what we
thought was the end.

MIRROR

My fate to meet my eyes where I'd meet yours,
 this early morning streaked with soot
mottled where your dreaming hand should put
my hand to rest on your still waking brow
jibing the night's storm-battered prow
heaven's third power, that makes another fast
be one of two, then, the scow safely moored—
(eyes shut) wish that was for me first be last.

ORBIT

je vais voir l'ombre que tu devins

—MALLARMÉ

That evening when you were standing by
the shelves and song came back to you after
a long silence, never broken even once
but for a shadow crossing your path, a murmur
of some long-ago breath, speeches as nursery rhymes,
St. Crispin or the children chanting, *please you,*
night and day, or the stained glass of the bay
as it opened for you when the tide rose
to meet the twilight. But never asking for you,
who had become a bystander, salt caked
by salt to a pillar and even then slipshod
with the truth. That swerving eel whose charge switches
the current is you, not another, slick
tail—remorse—caught in its own mouth.

*

The house a shell and not a shell. Dreaming,
I stop at each turn of the stair, kite
winder, the balustrade's tipped ladder tracking
infinity, each door a lid shut tight
my damp snail foot, proboscis, wrack fishtail.
How can I swim up so many stories?
On the landing, furs. Gloves. A walking stick,
Grandfather in his overcoat, clearing
his throat, the winter smell of carnations.
I tried to write it down but lost. Missed tread.
Footfall of what the dead said. Don't, or do?
All ear, I have no hands. Lunatic hero,
the hermit crab who keeps me company
turns me over, nebulae, on my back.

*

All day a playing card at the kitchen stair's hairpin,
seven diamonds, each red gem a step, Mnemosyne's
daughters, sun-sprockets, whirring to make you *listen.*
On a sequined pillow from Bombay, our Una's
papoose doll sits up beneath *The Book
of Justice,* a pop-up fugue whose page unfolds
a toothpick temple, each strut a reliquary,
its cellophane banner sheer petroleum.
By midnight, the card picked up: tears, doom-bringer,
futility: the owl asking its question
to the barking of dogs. Rusks and cardamom.
If Chronos comes to Hecate's door, what use
is squabbling? Yew-eyed, the cat mews the stair,
her footprints red after she steps on glass.

*

Dusk. Bee's *Sea of Monsters* butts the chair—
its shiny cover wreathed with lashing tails
while eight steps up, the kite winder, littered
with gilt ribbons, sails into Whitehall's helter-
skelter. I sit "on the stares." Fight or flight?
Downstairs, on pink ice, powdered ginger
spackles the Victorian mold's flutes with gold,
red lily pollen, prodded, makes us all
Macbeth. Tonight's story? Trawling for loot,
wan Elnora, "A Girl of the Limberlost,"
pulls from her torn pocket a scrimshaw boy,
a locket, a painted top—each butterfly
she nets a flustered treble note. We're not
good at being good, nor being *"good-at."*

*

The fireplace log breathes fire, pooled amber,
bejeweled topaz lighting a goblet. The air
is sap. Dragon, the pine log shatters to
a monkey face, two knots for eyes, then—gone.
What else eats itself alive? The child, not
eating, rattles her shark spine, wind chimes
for Belsen's banging door that only shuts.
North, the smudged mill towns carbonize, each one
dilated, black iris beneath the day's
cloud-muddied brow, horizon's dorsal fin
snow grey, as if the flooded dawn held dusk,
the shark's inamorata sunset's skinned
knuckle try at holding fast—gunpowder
sky that drinks smoke from an hourglass.

*

Each one Echo (spitting image of Narcissus
in diminuendo), the seven sisters play
bridge on their upside-down card table,
their meteor go-cart running on a firecracker.
Their swaged tablecloth is the snow sky settling
on the dark town. Who could do wrong? The eye
of the world opens and shuts. Remember
the legs under the table, silk and suede,
pine bark, sharp hooves, clattering? We spoke
in whispers, hardly breathing—house of cards
where every breath disturbs the dreaming portraits.
Shuffle the deck. The prince's tiny twitching
dog is dreaming us: dust and ore, secret, alive,
animal, just past vision's humming line.

*

Why can't I want anything I want? But,
Cosmo, I do. Posthumous, our loves
outlive us: hardtack, lemons, sassafras,
soap-skiff floating in the clawfoot tub,
the windlass a girl blowing bubbles.
Would that we'd known? A whitened cloud
of peppered moths, the children's old *de teum*
dims the lamp, singes the too-light evening
and turns the sky's slashed moiré tangerine.
I bartered forty summers for black pearls—
the cat's black tail, scorch mark, rounds the kicked
shut door. On Wings Neck two deer eat and graze.
I slip and water slops the stairs. Where I am
met is meat. What we knew we know was there.

*

The light through the wicker chair makes star-crossed
diamonds on the coffee cup, each watery
crystal quartz alit tells lies or makes
things up. What will I do with my life?
Rolled up the map of Angers—*somewhere else*—
resists, its antique blue print paper folds
an origami house on fire, its routes
and rivers set ablaze, the blown up center—
court, steeple, winding stair—a burnt out
        charcoal spyhole. Between the lines? In
the kitchen of the dragon king, the hooked carp,
speaking, has one wish: life as we know it.
Know-nothing, the curling paper serpent
sheds his printed skin but leaves me mine.

*

Tea-smoked duck on a sugar stick, at
the restaurant where in the dream I changed
tables and changed tables. Everything M. gave me
was a box—a glass box with pink transparent sides,
        a cloisonné *parfumerie.*
Do you want these boots? the dream said. I walked for miles
through racks of shoes, among the voodoo dolls—
but those are Martin's, I said. But who is Martin?
Then woke—*I am half turned away*—to rain,
and didn't think, a meal half-cooked, the stove aflame,
duck legs puckered running red, the cat left out all night
drenched and I—*you don't think,* who have failed
everyone I love, my hair a fright wig
        my heart a bat that bangs its head.

*

Shellacked with ice, the street a cracked snow globe
whose magic pool drips serum. Mystery or venom?
Reading aloud in our cocoa-cum-coffee cloud,
Miss Stanton, stepdaughter of Woking, Surrey,
drops her veil. It's not sorrow she feels, but terror,
then comedy—the bull butting his maze
of twigs, the baboon rattling the bedroom door.
Is love labor? *Pacem,* heart-ease. Our shadows
slip. In the ashram's hand-thrown toffee bowl
(*our guru has a sweet tooth, he likes M&Ms*)
the narcissus, one-eyed, strains against
its makeshift chopstick stake to bloom. My pen,
leaking, blots and counts to ten, its indigo
dilation drawing water rings on the ceiling.

*

Ships' time, the East River's septet of islands,
each triangle mast raised to a tin star.
The wind settles. Scant block from the cold bank,
my love, bell-ringer at ten, at five, star-hive,
diminishes to a speck, the wind's fugue
tripling her internal rhyme. That watermark
white quartz I kept, Mab's stone, whose ripples
whet the air her horses reined, her rune her wand,
your eye for mine—your taloned verses held
small birds in air until they sang. When you
turned to speak I bit my tongue and thought
not mine. Come to me now. Heaven's geometry
is hesitation's proof; the triangle's sharp
note—tin hitting crystal—makes us stop.

The cranberry bogs—plush seats at La Fenice,
but the sky's aria after weeks of rain?
Bee sting, a swarm of buttercups, mercury
monogrammed with fever. Three wishes?
Even the simple know to ask for more—
the baby's hand a star, the blinded
measuring snake a Möbius strip. Whom did Clotho
strangle but herself? Too many things
are possible in this world, Lachesis.
Fall is summer's bronze wing, it soars, then dips.
          Even Atropos is unpredictable—
a knife makes a fiddle of a breastbone,
a torn field mouse flicking rubies. My life
be my life, scarecrow punting at the moon.

*

Transit of mist, the blistered, peeling trees—
ice in the doorway makes us slip
and grab the brass knob that will and will not
turn. To choose a book is to choose—what?
Mrs. Dalloway, by the telephone,
steps out and shuts the door, the sky above Hyde Park
rickracked with clouds. Slight wind. Boot lifted above
a rainbow puddle. Do you remember?
We took a stick and twirled the gutter's oily
pond until the colors parted, Joseph's
coat, ragtag, the early sunset's bagatelle.
Love, if I could look at you—our life bleeds
into every corner; the sky's lavender lozenge
window, future tense, stores everything we do.

*

What rainbow amounts to anything?
The bracelet's lanyard on my wrist—woven
manacle, one a summer, *for mama*—
faint blush of mold on the sky's scud rim,
the horizon a bird blind high above Longnook
all bluff, the dune bowling down meteors,
its fatal hollows scored by falling timber,
spawn ghostwriting the low-tide mark.
Where are my happy loves? Right from wrong,
the simple past, asperity a rough
Venus, a mermaid and her twin seal
self, the blood red wax that stamps the letter
a welt on her fern tail, an x marking
          the spot where the light was.

SUMMER

for Max Ritvo

I

Three weeks until summer and then—what?
Midsummer's gravity makes our heads spin
each hour a gilt thread spool, winding through
the second hand, gossamer *fin de semaine,*
fin de siècle, fin slicing the water
of the too-cold-to-breathe bay, molten silver,
then receding as if we hadn't seen it,
sultan of *so long, see you tomorrow.*
      Dead man's fingers, lady's slippers, a seal
who swims too close—too close for what? The needle
swerves. Our element chooses us. Water
fire, air, earth—the rosebush, Lazarus,
hot to the touch, gold reticulate, is love's
bull's-eye, attar rising from the rafters.

I I

If I could make it stop I would. Was it
the crocodile Hook feared, or was it time?
The hour's arrow never misses, the gnomon,
glinting, cuts the Day-Glo sun to pieces.
In the ultraviolet palace of the Mermaid King
his girls wear scallop shells, one for each year
on their turquoise tails. Even they have birthdays,
why not you? Death, hold your ponies with one
hand, and stay awhile. On my desk, the lion's

paw lamp scavenged from the winter beach,
its poppy-colored shells like the lit scales
of an enormous Trojan fish . . . teeth chattering,
its metronome time bomb *tsk tsk*—
when is giving up not giving in?

III (CHILD'S POSE)

When Alice pulled the stopper, did she get
smaller, or did the world get larger? In
the bath, your nose bleeds a bouquet of tissue
roses, white stained red—adolescence
is to overdo it, but really? Thirty
stories up, our birds'-eye view is
the hummingbird tattoo on your bare head,
wings beating, too tiny and too big to see,
your wire-thin profile drawn upright, bones
        daring the air, marionette running on
the brain's dark marrow, tungsten for the fireflies'
freeze tag. Due south, the Chrysler Building's gauntlet
holds a lit syringe. We do and do not change.
Let me go from here to anywhere.

IV

That's it for now. And so we turn the page
your poems standing in for you, or—that's

not it, what's left of you, mediating
between what you'd call mind and body
and I, by now biting my lip, call grief,
        the lines netting the enormous air
like silver threads, the tails of Mr. Edwards's
spiders with which they sail from ledge to branch
"as when the soul feels jarred by nervous thoughts
and catch on air." *Pace*. Your trousers worn
to mouse fur dragging on the stoop, your hip
prongs barely holding them aloft, the past
a phaeton, its sunlit reins bucking
at before and after, but there is no after.

V

Or is there? For once, when you rock back
on the chair I don't say *don't do that*,
forelegs lifting, hooves pawing the air—
Every departure's an elopement,
the shy cat fiddling while Rome sizzles,
spoon mirror flipping us upside down.
        Son of Helios, rainbow fairy lights
blazing, when one light goes out they all
go out. At the top of the dune, the thorny
crowns of buried trees, their teeter-totter
branches a candelabra for the spiders'
silvery halo of threads. What a terrible
business it is, saying what you mean.
        Speak, sky, the horizon scored by talons.

STILL LIFE (FOR ROSE)

The purple pansy lion face circumspect
in the sweetheart roses' papery clutch

the day-old flowers' pale face powder scent
—I'm so old, I'm eighteen, it's downhill—

Rose on her birthday a down duck, chaff
won't stick, nor lies, nor love unless

she wills it so. The horizon's wishbone
snaps in two. We live on an island, although

you can't tell—Islamabad is in Pakistan,
the moon is blue, your hawk feather

a weathervane pointing north and south.

ANXIETY

Cat claws on the heart's tin roof, each breath
a locomotive running off the rails,
the switching signal's warning rat-a-tat
I'm up too early, the alphabet net snags
and tears, moths, then motes, then gone. What I love,
I undo, eye for eye, tooth for tooth.
No one knows me, matchstick Guy Fawkes doll,
my burnt head micro-ember sunset gleams,
day moon hostage to the dark's slant dream.
What ghosts I have I won't or can't give up.
Impossible to love or leave, poor self
banging its head, wanting—what?
As if I knew what I meant or wanted,
baby voice humming: mouth skull smile.

THE IMPULSE WANTS COMPANY

for Troy Schumacher and Ellis Ludwig-Leone

I

Funnel of trees, bees, corkscrew
   pines, the sky a map with a gold badge,

less wind where the grass is bent
     but the waves a white hedge—

        fanfare-breaking, curling under. Torque.
Froth. When we were children we came
     to the beach every day and ran

      down the high dune
to the water.
     I was a water nymph
there was a hole in the bucket
    we ran—

        somersault—

II

Seesaw. The green world
white and blue, salt-stripped—
   too big, sky too far, the sweet air

    —bright cartwheel the dune rolling over itself
     hurry—the sandpiper

leaves a snakeprint
    in the sharp sand

our scales shine in the wet sun
    flipping
        —a quick dolphin

its flank silver slicing the water
        pulling the swimmer
into the blue distance like a gaze.

The wind cocks its ear—
    a steady hum, the gills
        of the day opening

and shutting, sheen reflection
        a dream of summer

    —toe in the water—

umbrella a sunflower,
your body unfolding

        —blade-bone
          wrist hip

    the sand turning
    its toes under,

    the sun a pinhole
camera. Shadow.

III

The letters swim—*You said*
that wasn't it—

I meant—

it's too hot to fight too bright.
    Have you been in? Are you going

        in? Come on! Oh leave me
    be—You're the water rat,

you're the spoilsport,
    Watcha looking at?

Seahorse, minnow, crab claw,
    Neptune a phoenix, horsing
around—*All winter I dreamed*
    of the beach

        and here we are
    lizards—when I think—

a walk? *On this beach*

the girl I was lengthening
    and shortening her shadow
        hammered to silver—

    a shape in the sand far out.
        I see a boat, a cloud, they are
            waving from the boat—

He never goes in. *Why*
      is it such a big deal?
The impulse wants
    company.

        Out in the water the whales
   sing their beautiful warnings
      blue fire lit in water, the sand

infinitesimally sinking as the water

rises, the earth itself the selkie
      half-human, in love
with herself who returns

IV

to the sea, quaking, salt stars
on her skin, each one
     a Catherine wheel, pirouette,

a tiny galaxy, its
      Möbius strip
   giving the selkie back—
        slick
    dangerous—to herself

and others. *She'll be the death of me.*
      But he puts on her spangled cloak
   and drifts out or actually

paddles, selvage between air
    and water indistinguishable
     —hair, feather, scale, fin—

until he is smaller then gone but
        gigantic, the waves and
                the sea cradling him until he

lets go, cells sequins
        sloughing off, distilled
                swallowed

by the sea which is a whale
            made of sky.

            The dream which is
                    dry land inside out

swallowed

so that the scene on the beach—
        telling the story of
                a disappearance, a frisson,

v

life opening to swallow someone

        who gave no sign

really, it can happen anytime
        with so little provocation,
                disaster, the stars

misaligned, or set straight
in a way that was impossible to
        imagine, standing as we do

with our hands shielding our eyes
        to block the sun,
                is it the beach

which is drowning, the lover
        who wants to get away
                drowned by leaving

alchemical,
        regretting
                what was always

going to happen, a crescendo
        which is only natural
                when we think about loss—or

                        what passes for it
leaving the others—terrestrial
        incapable of leaving, then gone—

(Coda)

The dream of an ending
        the reluctant swimmer returning—

in a space carved from shadow and air
        dusk phosphorescent, a moonshell

fish, dolphin, minnow bird-bright blue—

    Shark

THE MUSE OF HISTORY

I   CLIO

let my tongue cleave to the roof of my mouth

    The past's fantasia cannot hold or let
us go. Flycatcher catching itself in
the pool's glint gaze, Samarkand where Tamerlane
hewed his bloody thread, unspooling across
the hacked-to-pieces field, a triple axle
splitting Clio's cataract, muddy then
clear, the opal of a rain-sheened open
eye that looks at nothing but yet holds
our look.
               Euterpe, my head is in my hands.
Flies speckle the field. The sizer, hissing,
straps dynamite to a waist no bigger
than a fly's wingspan, but the daughters
of Babylon do not tarry—the road flares
burn blue, bog irises, erect, quivering.

II   CHARLESTON

How shall we sing the Lord's song in a strange land?

The coiled snake sheds and eats itself, its bitten
tail an omphalos, the arrowhead's
stung fire hitting the scorched bull's-eye,
the crooning singer stopped mid-note, his silent
measure hung in air, a pillow slip, cotton

turning to cloud, immeasurable—
the President, singing.
                    At Appomattox,
when General Lee said to Ely S. Parker,
a Senecan, who recorded the terms
of the surrender, "It is good to have
a real American here," he replied, "Sir,
we are all Americans." The century
folds, a white flag rent with frazzled tears.
Let my demons rage so I know who they are.

III THE GONE WORLD

O daughter of Babylon

The calico licks each knuckle to a moonscape,
her velvet pupils two quotation marks.
          What's the opposite of oxygen?
Pure carbonation, the children trail their cartoon
balloons past where last night, sleepless on
my duck blind–barge, I steered the ragged sofa
across Persia's raveled coast and ran aground.
Cat and fiddle, dish and spoon, their voices
tinsel, threading time's slit-eye needle—
Does the moon hold water? The moon, or our
idea of it? Shall I come kiss you? *Yes, please.*
Fugitive, the cut-throat sparrow captive
bangs its head and takes the future's measure,
an echo climbing Eurydice's stair.

IV   AT HOME

we hanged our harps upon the willows

Every moment's a time bomb. The scorpion
inside a cage of flame will strike himself,
two of them will kill each other, black
carapace glimpsed through the needle's eye.
The flame darting where you laid it down
is Giotto's circle lit with paraffin,
your halo full of whirring bees. Come, lost
one, out of the shadows—the children's
sparklers constellate the sequined lawn,
Orion's arrows pinning fallen stars.
No man meets me. I strut the stair, half-dare
myself to miss the tread, shy spider,
all hands and legs—*If you don't see me,*
you ain't gonna have to wonder why.

V   INSIDE OUT

(for Michael Vincent Miller)

If I forget thee, O Jerusalem

Say what you see. I see a door. *A door?*
Is it open or closed? It is opening.
No, it's closing. Now it's closed, I think.
I think it's closed. *Where is the door? What*
sort of door is it? An inside door,
the door of a room. *Which room?* When
I was a child. A slipper of light.
But it's the wrong door! *Is there another door?*
When Charlemagne invited Alcuin

of York to Aachen to supervise the new
clear handwriting of God, the herded letters
jumped the fence like lambs. Moss on the door,
the hinges rusted shut, damp green on green.
I put my ear to it, the thick plank vibrating.

THREE POEMS

Fragment

Quiet descends.
       In a room full of steam the laundress
    is folding a sheet, a sail in fog,
  as when in midday far off, the shore turns north
  and shrouds itself in mist, and I said
    see, the cloud takes us too although
      we cannot see it, my skin cold to the touch
  but your blood beating under your shirt cuff
      the bat wing silk vibrato

      as when with the compass's bent arm
you drew a circle, your head bowed over it,
    shielding the paper, and inside the circle
the spoke of a wheel—the edge of a door
    swinging shut over the lintel that parsed
  the radiant light in pieces, whittling it
like a sailor, the light under
       his blade a soap doll coming to life
     as it is cut. In the middle

      of the night you were far off, beloved
in the shadows, and I—forgotten in
  that fold of sleep, death no longer so distant,
ready to provide an ending to a story
    if the speaker is at a loss, a black dog, a pyre of stones,
     a car scraping the side of the *strada*
  the paint scored, a lost child—at a standstill.
    See how we are caught,
      bees in the paperweight,

as I am, here, now in a circle of orange sunlight,
          listening to the birds'
cantata in the locusts by the driftwood arbor
       the sea unsnarled this morning
              by the wind carding the long
       white skeins of the waves
     the grapes not yet ripe although we are past
       midsummer, night and day
just touching, a ribbon of cold in the leaves.

The Fogbow

A day of offshore weather, the wet cove
overhung with elms, the sun cocooned
in cloud, the waves scrolling under and over.
We talked among ourselves. You read *Tartuffe*.
"In winter," you said, "in Frankfurt when I can't sleep,
I think of this sound." Heavy, foam-flecked,
two sleek-headed seals, their whiskers broom bristles,
bobbed not ten feet away. Your finger checked
the damp page of your book. When we next looked,
not a rainbow but a fogbow over the water—
a silver pencil line inside the sky's margins,
a circumflex that marked the barely there
that quickened us as if we'd seen a ghost
in the picture the fog had drawn in air.

Letter in Fog

In the late afternoon fog
moved in from the beach over
the landscape, down the road, and
onto the porch. The birds were
quite loud outside, or were they

inside? It was hard to tell,
the terns and a whip-poor-will,
and I could hear the frogs too,
or the horned toad, for we were
all in the cloud together,

the birds, the frogs, the maples,
and the porch where I was on
the long damp settee. Outside,
the green wet leaves pressed against
the still silver sky as if

they were printed, delicate
fronds of branches, the locusts like
coral set in tiny squares—
that was the screen—a kind of
grid painting, an afterimage

of a scene painstakingly
transferred, like a negative
developed in mercury,
the leaves' light radial spines
the creases of a hand held

up to a lamp, its lilac
bones like a starfish pulled from
the fog by a fishing pole.
It was true. I could barely
see my hand in front of me.

The fog was a cloud and we
were in it—the birds, the frogs
and the trees, the hand with its
blue, transparent, barely there
capillaries—suspended

in gelatin, inside out,
a sonogram, its huge head
full of mute wavery dreams.
I had a baby small as
a hazelnut and I knew

I must be careful not to
lose it; you dove from a high
bridge, straight down, not looking. Look!
The fog stayed for another
hour or so, and then was gone.

JAPANESE POEMS

Between the bent boughs
of the splayed sumac the silver
owl rests his head.

The perimeter
left by your absence is long
to walk in one day.

The angel in her
credenza of extreme beauty
dogs swim the river

I look for my heart
by the lamp where the light is
skitter in the wet black leaves

BLUE VASE

Because you like to sleep with curtains drawn,
    at dawn I rose and pulled the velvet tight.

You stirred, then set your hand back on my hip,
    the bed a ship in sleep's doubled plunging

wave on wave, until as though a lighthouse
    beam had crossed the room: the vase between

the windows suddenly ablaze, a spirit,
    seized, inside its amethyst blue gaze.

What's that? you said. A slip of light, untamed,
    had turned the vase into a crystal ball,

whose blue eye looked back at us, amazed, two
    sleepers startled in each other's arms,

while day lapped at night's extinguished edge,
    adrift between the past and future tense,

    a blue moon for an instant caught in its chipped
    sapphire—love enduring, give or take.

SUNDAY

I EARLY MORNING

The rain, gray god with its huge hands
has shredded the roses, and clapping
kept us up all night, the bridge washed out,
the troll waiting to gobble a goat.
How long has he been there, wet and cold,
            impatient, starving, his coat
rent with welts and matted with mist?

            Father, thundering, his voice full
of bracken and leaves, leaves that in
the autumn clogged the gutters. *Who
goes over the bridge? Who goes there?*
    the billy goats stammering, pawing
the air. But I am the goat and the troll,
and so cannot pass or grant passage.

I I

The high meadow filled with sweet grass!
The spindle puts the moon to bed,
the window latched, the sheets pulled tight,
pincushion star, ram butting his head,
my brother and sister behind and ahead—
his sister was no use to him either,
            she took what was his, cat's cradle

bridge made of sharp goats' thread. Who
goes there now, over the rickety
bridge? Tiny steps, lickety-split,
my place is in the pause between
        the thunder and the bridge, Father
shouting over the torn white water,
hoofprints mark the place last seen.

III   AT THE MUSEUM (BELLOWS)

(for Alexander Nemerov)

        The man in the left hand corner
of Bellows's picture of the Dempsey-Firpo
fight, the picture a dream, so not a real
fight—a picture of a fight—his flayed hide
just visible under his blue pinstripes,
the watcher and the fighter
        indistinguishable, one inside

the other, lion and lion tamer,
the paint daubs faces or fingerprints
and the lights staring and staring across
        the fretwork of the ring, and Bellows
himself, next to him, looking surprised,
as if to be there was to give himself up
without our noticing it, as we all do

in a gesture, or word, leaving something
behind we should have taken with us
        or even guarded, a way of not letting
something be over and done with.
The fight was over in four minutes flat.
A curious thing about the painting
is that Bellows chose to show us

the moment when Firpo sent Dempsey
careening, with a blow to the jaw,
one of the two times he laid him out,
and we, with the spectators crammed
        into the foreground of the picture,
have to help push Dempsey back
into the ring where two-and-a-half

minutes later he will defeat Firpo,
who went down four times to his two.
In Assisi, at the Basilica di San Francesco,
        in the panel in which Giotto depicts
the moment Francis gives away
his worldly goods, the palm that Francis
raises up to the hand that is reaching

down to him from heaven, a hand out
of the blue, open, ready to give or
receive wonders, is the same hand
in Bellows's picture raised behind Dempsey—
        one wing of a dove, the impulse is
to press our own palms to it, and despite
our better judgment, to hurl him back.

IV   BLACKBIRDS

A song that Father liked to sing:
    a dozen blackbirds baked alive
but still alive when they did bring
    the pie to set before the king—
what a flurry when the pie was cut!
    The birds cawed madly as they rose—
blackbirds flapping blackened wings
    who circled back to snip your nose!

I see the moon, the moon sees me,
shining on the apple tree . . .
    don't sit under the apple tree
with anyone else but me—
    no, no, with anyone else but me . . .
sound of hurry, over the bridge.

V AT THE MUSEUM (WYETH)

    As always, we want something from the dead,
even the blackbird, stiff in a kind of grassy net,
    its black leather gangster feet curled up
as if holding on to something it let go—
    and beyond, to the right, inevitably, a house—
black-shuttered with its high gray wing,

    its bones buried deep in the earth like a beast
that once took flight, bones with the imprint
    of feathers, that print repeated in the faraway trees
on a rise to the left of the house, a good distance
    away, as if the trees had been painted by pressing
a painted leaf to the canvas, the spine

    the tablature of a feather, or fish, the scales
clearly marked in miniature, although we know
    the trees are much bigger than the blackbird
so stock-still in the spiky grass, so lately landed,
    its glossy mourning coat spit-shined. Under
those trees, a short distance from the house

    as nowhere else in the picture, a moment
of repose, the sun on the warm bark, the circle
    of cool beneath. But the bird holds us fast,
a shadow cast by moonlight, the flowers

beside it articulate as the delphiniums
in *La Primavera,* at the Uffizi, at which we

paused until we could look no longer at
an extreme propensity for beauty, as though it
        might explode in smithereens. Autumn,
the seedpods are moth-eaten moons, dry, rattling.
        In Wyeth's more famous picture, the girl
stranded in the foreground in a clutch of weeds

her awkward limbs stretching in the hissing grass
is in the same place in the picture plane
        as the blackbird, we all agreed with this,
the woman in the white hat—why a hat,
        inside the museum, and her friend, smaller,
dressed all in black, black shoes, black stockings,

black dress, although it is summer.
At once we want to help her as she reaches
the unbridgeable distance of the field
        and the meadow filled with rough grass
although it's not so evident how to help her
        for even now our heavy limbs twitch with

enchantment, caught by a dream in which
it is impossible to move except by slithering.
        In my sleep you said I said—*too many people.*
The black house is a ship on the horizon,
        every light on, or the moon that looks
as if it is following us but from which

we are always veering away, the white wolf
snapping at our heels, goading us to cross
        the bridge or waiting for us by the water
its white face wavering under the pilings.

The girl is a blackbird in the high grass,
it is natural to mistake one for the other

when it is so difficult despite the painter's
efforts, herculean, really, to see clearly—

VI   SATURDAY NIGHT (AT THE BALLET)

Puck, above a game of flashlight tag
the tiniest fairy pirouetting like a dervish—
the honeysuckle wood alit, one pointed
green-shod foot dangling, like the hand that reached
down to Francis to pull him up to heaven
or rebuke him, or the white hand coming
out of the darkness over the ring: counting
one, two, three, alley, alley, innisfree—
the three goats balking at the bridge, Father
bellowing over the rushing water
the river loud, rearing its head, foam rushing past
its eyes and ears, Father clamoring, needing
something—the moment we know
            it has come to nothing.

VII   (THE DREAM)

The heavens shift.
And presto! the tilted abacus
of stars slides back in place, twilight's worn edge rubbed
to a sheen. Queen, ass, Indian child, love-lit quartet, slipping
    as the constellations do
            behind Gaia's unearthly tilt
        leaving us in night's cooler, less demanding air
                where our taxi driver has his phone
on speaker: twenty minutes of harangue,

a hornet trapped inside a troika, the driver
 silent except once to say,
interrupting the ceaseless string of epithets,

 "You are the woman of my dreams."
 The avenue slick before the curb,
lights turn from red to green. Remember? The crescent
moon scar on my knee—

 Rain patters the windshield, the lights
 from the bodega spatter lime and pink.
 A folded scene.
 Above, the moon—
 another night before a halt.

VIII   EVENING AND MORNING

Morning lit by evening's lantern, the cat
a baby falling from the broken bough,
childhood's terrible litter of fear.
I am the goat and the goat is me. I see the moon,
the moon sees me. And if I die before I wake,
the spirit leaving the body as we sleep
as Giacomo said in the gospel—who said it, where?
if the spirit leaves my body where does it go?
—and in the dark the pine knots watching
and your eyes big in the dark, and the sound of breathing.
In your sleep you said *too many people.*
I woke you in the dark and I took you by the hand—
How far is the moon? If I folded this piece of paper?
But then you would never get there, remember?
And your total disregard of me—
Twilight's rainbow a lasso fetching the moon from the water.
When I was walking I fell from the curb.
You did not. *I did, I did.*

The three children not far off
cross the road to the water
and into the hot high grass,
their feet light on the flattened
stalks of the cattails that line
the swale like pale raffia
woven expressly for that

purpose, as if the landscape
was a diorama made
of glassine, straw, and folded
paper. Whose children are they—
one, two, three, walking to
the ruined, silvery, splintery
boat, that looks like a whale come

ashore in the pocket cove
which opens at high tide like
a giantess's compact?
There is another smaller
shadow, pulling a kite—or
no, a pull-toy dog, which barks
at an upturned horseshoe crab

and a stained, eyeless, gray-brown
gull. How oddly sound travels
over water. Underfoot
the sun-crazed hermit crabs run
helter-skelter to their bomb
shelters under the wet sand,
where at dead low tide the marsh

makes a kind of long humped bridge
of itself to the rapt cove
and the ruined quiet. *Psst* says
the wind. The children run at
it, lowing their heads, making
horns with their fingers, bashing
themselves in it and through it.

X CASE SENSITIVE

Two days I've forgotten where I'm going,
New York's crossword up and down a litter
of numbers and letters. I spin on the grid,
round hole in a square peg, each step a rope
bridge hung in air, my tongue a troll who eats
my words, my goat-fur cloak held fast by Psyche's
brooch. "Smile, libling, you have your whole life
ahead of you." *Hold on tight.* Even the dead
won't speak to me, my sharp hooves beating
the bank's slick grass, the bog oak's muddy rune.
Bee disheveled on the stairs, the storm
rattling the panes. *"I dreamed I walked and walked
and could not find my way."* Dear God, let me
keep my dreams to myself and do no harm.

DEAR AND BLACKBIRDS

e tu allor li priega
per quello amor che i mena, ed ei verranno

—DANTE, *INFERNO*, CANTO V

One by one they walk down
the fence of trees by the swimming pool,
  delicate endearments, their hooves

just printing the dew-drenched lawn
with arrowheads. From the long table
  where months ago we ate

breakfast, they are just visible,
the small things we say to each other—
    ti penso e ti bacio

written in the cold grass, that if we were
barefoot would pierce our feet.
    The other morning, early,

on Broadway, when you must admit
it was a miracle we were still
        standing—we were rushing

there was no time for anything—you said
"this weather is perfect" and raised
        your shirt to let the faint chill

touch your skin, and I grazed
my hand over it, feeding like a blackbird,
    un corvo, un uccello nero,

a raven, which can be one who
is ravenous, the word, translated, *caro,*
      windblown for once into flesh.

YOUR MOTHER DANCING
ON THE TABLE (FIESOLE 1966)

In the long low living room
after everyone has gone,
your mother in a sleeveless
shift dress made out of some stiff
      turquoise material
is dancing on the table.

      It is a cold night. She is
not wearing stockings. She has
kicked off her shoes. In her bare
feet, long arms aloft, she is
      conducting Mozart, which
streams from the turntable

      to the stereo speakers,
then eddies, waves lapping the
huge untidy room, where she
is just now beautifully
      alone for one minute.
Upstairs you and your sister

      are asleep. Your grandmother
is reading in the next room.
It is the year the Arno
flooded. Your grandmother's own
      house is underwater.
Her bookmark is embossed with

a crescent moon C, her own
watermark. Her earrings are
diamond clips. Her feet are dry.
Her neighbors were rescued from
        their roofs and pulled from their
windows. What's that noise? you asked

        your sister. She is six, she
is two years older, she can
read; in her white nightgown she
is a dandelion. You
        are not asleep—really, it
is early evening, not night

        at all. You are playing a
game with counters, she has the
shoe and you have the hat, and
you run down the hall to fetch
        your grandmother, who puts
down her open book and in

        stocking feet walks downstairs with
you and your sister. The word
you use when you tell me this
story is *accomplices,*
        in the language that first
belonged to your mother and

        now we use between us. In
the living room at the foot
of the stairs your mother was
still dancing, her body a
        tuning fork, conducting
the music. Stop it! your sister

cried out, and tried to shield you
so you would not see. "Don't be
so puritanical," said
your mother, a word that your
            sister did not know but
in the language in which your

            mother spoke to her, she heard
a word she both did and did not
not know, a bad thing, and she
began to hit your mother on
            the legs, to make her come
down from the table, as the

            tide of sound roared under her.
Outrageous! your grandmother
said—she'd always known about
your mother and here was proof!
            Your black hair was damp from
your bath. Your light blue cotton

            pajamas were buttoned to
the neck. Your body was sleek
as a badger's, a body
to which nothing much had yet
            happened, the secret life
of the body that occurs,

            to us and in us in small
increments, fiercely, subtly,
as it did the afternoon
you told me this story—but
            even then you knew you
had never seen anything

more beautiful than the sight
of your mother dancing on
the table, Mozart coursing
under her above
the flooded city, through
the open shutters into

the green twilight, as when the
angel said to Tobias:
see the fish flashing in the
river. Half a century
later, six stories up,
blocks from the Hudson, you say

to me, I missed you, I had
music on before people
came and I was dancing. Now
you ask me to listen to
you and I do, and what
I hear is the sound of your

mother's bare feet keeping time
as she danced on the table,
the high notes her hands, quick stars
in quickened air, the music—
the moment before she
stopped and after it.

METAPHYSICKS

I METAPHYSICK FOR THE NEW YEAR

If Love would have her way with us
    she'd bind us lip to brow and brow
to knee, and wind a lariat
        of leaves about Love's moment that
in it holds all time. But you
        and I are sick of love. The year
has turned. My heart, where nothing sat—
    a wreath Love bound, that by our will
        will prove a collar or a crown.

II A WEEK LATER

If as we'd thought: once monthly thus
for three decades, this twelve-month near
   used up our quote of days, and squared
that dozen though the year, a hoop,
    swerved summer—zero sum, that season's
      integer, when lost we pared
then doubled nought as if to reckon
    absence out of air. As if minus
        made Love's quotient disappear.

III   MID-JANUARY

"Indeed, it is the first day again and again of everything."

In deed each day is made anew—
        Time's gaze in time turns trespass true;
Love's tempered arrows hit and miss
        and hit their mark, and prick out words
the blind by touch can read. For when
    birds touch down upon a pond's blue
  eye, by concentric rings its iris
widens. Time, sit by Love's side.
        The night unfolds tomorrow's news.

IV   TO HERSELF, DIMLY

These verses that you write, what mean
        you by them? Love not chatter needs
as swans bemoaneth not more white
        to bleach their plumes but beg instead
a pond where they might preen. Smirking,
        you purport: she makes her own, for
sturdy craft whose bowsprits export
        spume. But Love regards not shirking.
            On her own heart she feeds.

V   A GAME OF CHESS

A board atilt between two chairs.
      How long, Love asks, has this gone on?
In dream patois will mimics whim—
   the Queen remits her bracelets, viziers,
    wits, and pawns her heart to colonize
the King, who retreating draws in air
     a triad now become a square.
On which he sits. Radiant, Love
      pulls that throne from under him.

VI   RIDDLE

Cat fur on end means a back up;
     two crossed sticks may coax a flame;
smoke can blind or make Love fly away
   though ardor magicks smoke to fog
       and Love to Fool, who remarks not
  an unmade bed when Folly says:
      lie down on it. The pussy willow's
rune is spring. Now spell your name—
   wert gone (but stay!) in winter's pillow.

VII   JUPITER IN RETROGRADE

The end of winter's transit moon
    brings woe. So does a horse, bedazzled,
  stay its trot, else run too hot
and called cantankerous. Make not
  a twelve-month filly walk too soon—
    vexed, her legs will buckle under.
      Love bends a knee and bids the muzzle
graze; better fat abed then skint
abroad, lest hurry put asunder.

VIII   TALKING ABOUT IT

Hip, instep, knee, wishbone—bewitched.
  And every molecule sequined
until Love's skin becomes a suit
  of scales, each note a star that singing
makes no sound but breathing says—
  nota bene: there, and there, as musing,
Love makes of touch a pretty lute—
      nerve, my own, and tender pitch.

IX MONTHS LATER

As if Love's heart run out of air
    so as my heart too high would speak
so that my sleeve now a white flag
      that which simple made unstuck—flags
        at the chase. I thought I was other
  than I am. My busking hat? To
my betters, whose petitions wreak
        more havoc than I bring to bear.

X ANATOMY

If you court heartbreak you may marry
    it. Love balks, protests, grieves, tarries—
      The long way round a slipknot noose,
  no hanging, but had a heart ankle,
      wrist, knee (for though it be a living
        thing it does not walk, live, coo)—
Wrong. These many limbs in traction.
    For the heart do sup, cry, sleep, rankle.

XI CATHEXIS

If I could take my heart by stealth
and place it in my heel, so that
   my ribs might make a belfry where
        love's bell might forge anew a tongue—
   and then by walking so repair
        the newborn changeling to brute health
I'd whistle as I walked the route—
   or that's the tale I tell myself.

XII BURN

A dozen makes it come out right
but as a stone thrown in a pool
makes rings that perfect do not touch
so Love, exhausted, makes her rule—
   enough. But truth, restrained, unspools
   and spills. Hot water burn upon my breast
makes manifest my heart's remit,
   and my foot lame, where it was put.

CODA

Folly, to think rhyme could make stand
that at which Love throws up its hands.

ELBOW

Poggio, compass, hinge, spur-star,
   under my finger the worn knob
warm leather, wrinkled, a little
    rough, your elbow that has rested on tables
     —writing, eating, bringing a spoon
to your mouth, nudging the door open,
   skinned itself, folded itself
around me and others, the same
elbow that has been everywhere with you,
    so that I find myself jealous, even,
beloved in the early morning
   on this particular day in history
and here under my finger now!

CONVERSAZIONE

*Codesto solo oggi possiamo dirti,
ciò che* non *siamo, ciò che* non *vogliamo.*

—MONTALE

A small breath lifting the curtain,
    here, not *here,* now tell me which—
        and in the avenue Pasternak's

        snowflakes, white moths circling
    the Hudson's streetlamps, like my body
astral, touching yours in transit,

a bride's ghost veil, a white egret
    under a waterfall, and
        from a palazzo of clouds, a boy

        falling into your arms—
    a trumpet's adagio, and the
sound you make clearing your throat, a latch

opening, and I slipped through it
    alone though I did not know
        it then, the sound magnetized, the split

        song heard by a dog who
    would later be fed glass, cuttlefish
bones fed to the birds. I ate from

the hand I have made you almost
     wholly without your consent,
         and you walked to the river without

        me, warming my hands by
   blowing on them, the ceiling fan a
starburst shredding the air, the bed

Agostino's boat, octopus
     pots on the wharf, the bleached sheets
         puckering. *Don't you know I like storms?*

        Fifty blocks north, the snow,
   lace on the stoop, is sand blown in from
the desert where the red cow lows

and cries for her calf. *Mi manchi*
     perche non sei qui, these lines
         between tenses, one eye winked shut, far.

LATE AFTERNOON

Three pairs of binoculars but which one works—
why do we say "pair" when we mean one?
What we see is what we are—the swimming
pool's black shadow eye-mote, a mole, drowned,
its stiff bird feet a blurred ideogram.
Fetch the net. The day's stuck fast. Feverish
July, lilies mark the lawn, crimson
yellow, tangerine—a Palio, each bloom
a pony with its tongue mete out. Beyond
the big white tent, a giant's handkerchief,
the red-hot smokehouse writes its blue cursive.
When I was a girl, I made friends with a willow
and gave it the gift of my loneliness—
How near is near? How far is far?

CLASS PICTURE

I'm the eighth tallest. How do you know?
For the class picture, we stood in line.
When we were smaller I came third but now—
Dreaming my way that night back forty years
I saw, or thought I saw myself, one girl
in a staggered row of girls, tiers reaching up
astride a hill or bandstand, head turned
to speak into the ear of the next girl.
I felt my too hot shirt, my hank of hair,
my purposely averted gaze; I had
no friend but being not there, unrecorded
except by a gigantic eye, looking
down from a great mesmerizing height . . .
though I could not have said that then, or why.

OUIJA BOARD

for Langdon Hammer

A house with ghosts—or it should be. Wide planked
    floors, Limoges, a stop for oystermen and slaves,
salty dacha for a flyspecked Doge—all

topsy-turvy, bent off-course, weathervane,
    sundial, garden elves, if there *was* a course—
clams in the scuttle, a whale bone corset

keeping the ospreys from the chimney.
    walleyed gardener bending spoons. Rackety
spirits tucked up tight unhinge the scripted

shopping list: *buy six mobsters* and *let us.*
    Let us what? Heaven knows, to die in bed?
Not for us the dreamy seer of Athens

and her aperitifs—instead, a shriveled
    mermaid reading thrillers. When having tried
—post-beach—biking, a goat farm visit, and the swap shop,

I suggest the talking board (the day's loot?
    a hula hoop, five horseshoes, and a disco
ball: some things are best forgotten though it's hard,

lately, to remember which), the gang demurred:
    guests caught between the platform and the train
never, ever go away. And haven't we

got ghosts galore? Yours, mine, and ours, true
    believers all in mayhem and black magic—
pricking thumbs, portents, not courting trouble,

et cetera. Or rue the cost. (Our tab,
        unlike Jimmy's, won't extend to after-
hours drinks on Mars, though imbecile,

regrets a passing fancy, if it's passed,
        for a siren song turned pennywhistle.
Or so they do say—whoever they is.)

And so the new board stayed in cellophane
        stashed on the listing shelf beneath a gay
balsa model of the *Emily Ann,*

a spidery note fixed with old masking
        tape to its drag queen Barbie figurehead:
Gone to ground on Longnook Beach, 1710—

the year the harpooner's house was built. But
        in high weather the wind, Orion's tail, whips
and stirs the wakeful house into that doomed

revenant split ship, and us to dreaming
        sheeted sailors. There's no telling where we drown.
Why not here, lashed to the bedpost, going

down, down, down, the red Chinese wallpaper
        starred with seawater, the blue plates painted
with blue storm-tossed waves, foreshadowing the

captain's final call: *Ship's ahoy!*—all hands
        on the floating board, just barely touching
the ghostly writ in water A–Z,

    propelled by ghosts-in-waiting, as we are?

RAINY DAY FUGUE

The rain on the roof splits
into drops, one, then another,
a splatter of opals, and then
pools on the window ledge
where someone—when
was it?— left the mark
of a hammer set down
before the paint dried
to worn blue, the color
of the sky before it's fully
light, when it isn't raining.

Beneath the rain the quiet
is tremendous, hollowing out
the day that expands endlessly
one followed by another
and a third, indistinguishable,
from one another, a set
of moving mirrored shadows.
A diving bell from which, today,
it feels—unlikely—to emerge.
Outside, the rain sluices
down the bent azaleas,

pooling in the declivities
of the sharp flagstones
and the mossy spaces
between them. The rain comes
from far away, it is almost
impossible to imagine it,

the acres of cloud bound
over this part of the earth,
but even so a drop lands.
A blue diamond squirreled
in the cup of a leaf curling

on the parapet, a leaf from
the desiccated geranium.
Beneath the umbrella of the roof,
silence. The words of the book
swim, minnows in a stream
strung with gilt lozenges
from the reading light—
which clear only to wobble
again. What is it made of,
the lump in the throat—
feathers, or coal? Neither.

Or has the rain come,
somehow, inside?
It is tears. And the bird
outside the window who
seems not to know it is
raining, or for its own reasons
is pretending not to know,
sings one note, then another.
Or is it two birds, talking
together? The rain
knits itself on the long needles

of latitude and longitude
along the bridges and avenues
where the sodden leaves
make tracks of brown and gold
across the tarmac and clog
the gutters, the water rising
until the house, the walls,
the curtains printed with
rickshaws and flowers, your
sweater, are made of mist.
        Once years ago

I was riding a bicycle
on the hill and the blue
reared up at the bent arm
of the road and I thought
mountain, or *cloud.* It was
the sea, blue and gigantic,
a V of paint at the notch
of the turning. A friend
told me the other day
that for the tightrope walker
the most treacherous
moment is the turning,

reaching a destination
only to go back the way
he came. The rain
keeps its colloquy
on the roof. When it pauses

the birds make a tremendous
noise, beating their wings
as if to dry them, tracing
arcs in the damp air, as
if they had been waiting
keenly for this one moment

in which to make themselves
heard, white on white on
white, their beaks scribbling
and in the mind's cool
barely open eye the sky turns
itself inside out, seamlessly
reflected in water.
Or as the page does now
where beyond its wrought
iron fences, pools and hills

rise in a rain-soaked landscape,
both near and far, birds,
and what look like birds,
and small houses, their roofs
glistening, and the trees
heavy with water,
which we would see
if only once more we
could manage it—on
the page which for
this hour hasn't turned.

A story. Summer. I remember
bees in the clover, the vivid nasturtiums
climbing the speckled foxgloves, the smell
of shells lining the path, rot and seawater.
Wasps thrummed in the pine hollow,
the sun was so hot it could burn
a hole in paper if you put a glass to it.

          Inside the doorknobs
were too hot to touch.
The air was still. The birds I recall
were finches and wrens, you knew
the names of birds and I knew the names
of flowers. It was enough to go on.

This is a wrong turn. Start again.

A story. It is summer. Bees
in the clover. And I—what
was I doing, on the green hill?
Reading. I was reading
or pretending to read—
it is hard to tell at this
distance. Or to say what
I was feeling, though still
even now I see the birches
and hear the voice of the owl.
Tread lightly here. A hiss
in the grass. The mill

wheel turning the sleeve
of the sky. The other day
—it is thirty years later—
I came upon that paragraph
I was pretending to read
     that day on the hillside
the light strong through
the birches, the words—
the words darting.

     But she begged him to let
her alone, she almost pushed
him back; she drew Verena out
          into the dark freshness, closing
the door of the house behind her. There
was a splendid sky, all blue-black
          and silver—a sparkling wintry
vault, where the stars were like
               a myriad points of ice.

The letters worn, where my eyes
had grazed them.

I I I

What says the brown wren?
Be better off dead.
What says the jackanapes—
stand on your head.
What says the violet?

What says the hen?
If you don't love me
caulk the bucket, dull the blade
forget left luggage
left unclaimed
cat in the bag, cow in the barn,
quiet the bells,
what made you think
you could do me harm?

She'll die of hunger
say the geese in the pond.
A crown of beetles round her head,
Saucy puts herself to bed.
Star in the manger
hang it by the door—
if you come calling
I won't be there anymore.
Pinto pony gallops
by the ragged track
at a zebra crossing
you need to look both ways.
If you come back to me,
if you can find your way

the cat will say good morning
and open up the door.
The Appaloosa's hide
speckled brown and grey—
is it how he sees it,
that it got that way?

My head is in the oven
my heart has ruled my head
when you see me coming
I'll head straight away.
One hen lays white eggs,
the Araucana blue—
which one do you think
breaks my heart in two?

IV

The rain on the roof
ice in the eaves
and between, the up
and down lines, straight
and round, a tunnel
strung sideways. If
I put up my hands
the ivy strays, long
sentences, telling
stories. The rain
on the roof flushes
cold tears. Only
one bird, that I hear.
What does it say?
How long must I stay?

ACKNOWLEDGMENTS

Poems in this book first appeared in the following publications: "Sunday" in *Poetry;* "Japanese Poems" in *The Paris Review;* "Mirror," "Meltwater," "Dear and Blackbirds," "Flowers," "Faun," and "The Impulse Wants Company" in *Little Star;* "Metaphysicks" in *The Yale Review;* "Orbit" (sections I–VII) and "Conversazione" in *Agni;* "Letter in Fog" in *The American Scholar;* "Your Mother Dancing on the Table (Fiesole 1966)," "Class Picture," "Fragment," and "Ouija Board" in *Plume;* "Blue Vase," on poets.org (American Academy of Poets) and in *Monteverdellege* as "Vaso Azzuro."

"The Impulse Wants Company" and "Dear and Blackbirds" were commissioned by BalletCollective. Ballets based on these poems (choreography by Troy Schumacher, music by Ellis Ludwig-Leone) premiered in New York on August 14, 2013, and October 18, 2014, respectively. "The Impulse Wants Company" was printed by the Thornwillow Press for BalletCollective (2014) in an edition of 250 copies.

Frontispiece drawing made by Cynthia Zarin using Olafur Eliasson's drawing machine, *The endless study,* 2005, during the exhibition *Your waste of time,* neugerriemschneider, Berlin, 2006.

A NOTE ABOUT THE AUTHOR

Cynthia Zarin is the author of four previous collections, including most recently *The Ada Poems,* as well as a book of essays, *An Enlarged Heart: A Personal History,* and several books for children. She is a longtime contributor to *The New Yorker* and the recipient of fellowships from the Guggenheim Foundation, the National Endowment for the Arts, and the Ingram Merrill Foundation. A winner of the Peter I. B. Lavan Younger Poets Award and the *Los Angeles Times* Book Prize for poetry, she teaches at Yale and lives in New York City.

A NOTE ON THE TYPE

This book was set in Adobe Garamond. Designed for the Adobe Corporation by Robert Slimbach, the fonts are based on types first cut by Claude Garamond (c. 1480–1561). He gave to his letters a certain elegance and feeling of movement that won their creator an immediate reputation and the patronage of Francis I of France.

COMPOSED BY
North Market Street Graphics, Lancaster, Pennsylvania

PRINTED AND BOUND BY
Thomson-Shore Inc., Dexter, Michigan

DESIGNED BY
Iris Weinstein